Clyde–my river

G W Colkitto

Published by Cinnamon Press
Office 49019, PO Box 92, Cardiff, CF11 1NB.
www.cinnamonpress.com

ISBN 978-1-78864-130-2

British Library Cataloguing in Publication Data. A CIP record for this book can be obtained from the British Library.

Designed and typeset in Bodoni by Cinnamon Press. Cover design by Adam Craig.

Cinnamon Press is represented by Inpress Ltd.

Acknowledgements

'Diving Shipwrecks' was originally published in *Brantwood: that place of little green poems*, Cinnamon Press; 'Sunset: Arran' in *Looking Out*, anthology, Beautiful Dragons; 'With my brother at Largs' in *Family Too*, Dreich, and 'Millport—Wish you were here' on Lochwinnoch Station Platform as part of the Passing Time Exhibition,-Scottish Mental Health Arts and Film Festival 2019.

Contents

Source	11
New Lanark	12
Livingstone Birthplace Museum	13
Tourist Route	14
Glasgow Green	15
City Wharfs	16
Suspension Bridge	17
Finnieston Pedestrian Ferry	18
Pacific Quay—Garden Festival 1988	19
Gallowhill Road	20
Diving Shipwrecks	21
The Ferryman at Blythswood	22
Renfrew Ferry	23
A Renfrew Ferry Hogmanay	24
Tribute to The River Cart	25
Slack Water—Erskine Bridge 1969	26
Langbank	27
Bowling Harbour—1985	28
The Lady Anne	29
Greenock Esplanade	30
Bay Hotel Gourock	31
Wemyss Bay Station and Pier	32
With My Brother at Largs	33
On the Next Tide – Largs Marina	34
Arran Peaks	35
Seamill Shore	36
For the Silent Curlew of My Beach	37

Hunterston A from Millport, Nineteen-fifties 38

Millport—Wish you were here 39

Out-going Tide—Rothesay 40

Kilchattan—Isle of Bute 41

Jupiter 42

Holidays at Whiting Bay—Arran 43

At Lochranza Distillery 44

Sunset: Arran 45

Ailsa Craig 46

To my friends, who listen and encourage

Clyde–my river

Source

this springs into argument
competing places flow from the tongue
Tinto Hill, Daer Water, Crook Burn
which you believe does not matter to me
I never saw the need to trace
anything to its birthplace

when young I accepted what was
now age has restricted exploration
to what can be walked in least discomfort

anyway it's like trying to pin my foibles
on a great great grandparent never met
I never saw them or they me

so I never sat watching the droplets rise
from a straggle of moss or sparkle a rock
with ribbons of light but I know it is there
in the mists and myths.

New Lanark

it is always bright when I go
I choose the good days
New Lanark like a warm blanket
should wrap me in comfort
I feel a chill wind of reality
slide up from the river
benevolence of Dale and Owen
the lowest common denominator
tallied in bottom lines
of the industrialists
workforce delivered
better education better housing
reaped in output and higher profit
this model town I touch weeping
the river cannot drown

Livingstone Birthplace Museum

a snatched moment on the bridge
this day of sunshine
above the white swirls of the Clyde
from afar the sounds of happiness
children playing in the museum grounds

we laugh at your Brownies' misunderstanding
I am the bus driver who
Brown Owl has pulled on the journey

the mix of laughter and water
holds us above the gorge
hanging like a stopped clock
moments so sweet they never dissolve
time meaningless to the river
to love.

Tourist Route

meander of garden centres
tomatoes strawberries endless teas
down stream the cranes and funnels wait
here the river transforms from rivet and horn
to scent of green lullaby of water

the route takes me to memories of Dad
as we pass the Popinjay Hotel
I see him with the inevitable bible
held by elastic band, holding his faith

he was stopped on this road by the police
returning home from the work's Christmas Do
in the Popinjay police hoping for red-nosed revellers
to bag over the limit they pushed for proof of identity
from this abstainer to be given his bible
shown the dedication on the fly leaf.

Glasgow Green

Glasgow Green lay east
gangland of my mythic Admiral
I could not risk it

City Wharfs

fifties grey shoppers flood streets
bowler hatted trilby tipping office workers
trim secretaries hurry their lunch

I rush for steam grim train
leave the city behind
passing above the city wharfs

sheds swallowing timber
crates of vegetables swinging from holds
a puffer loads its strange shaped cargo

torpid river idles sludge brown
flow held by the surge of tide
sea and river in imperfect balance

the river shimmers oil rainbows
sewage scum waits its turn
to escape

Suspension Bridge

I thought it exotic
as if California came to Glasgow
wanted to paint it gold

Finnieston Pedestrian Ferry

I wait for Dad crossing on the small two ended craft which plies
between the rotundas of Finnieston and Govan. Below the river
lies the tunnel which carried goods, horses and pedestrians, but
as they had to descend and climb without the benefit of a lift, it
was quicker, less effort, to take the ferry. The river is muddy,
swirling, threatening and I think on my cousin, sometime bouncer
at The Barrowland Ballroom, caught out by the last ferry on Sundays
being earlier, stripping to his underpants, bundling clothes on his
head, like some wartime Chindit, and swimming across. Behind me
is Betty's Bar, which I was persuaded to enter as an experience for
three callow students. It was certainly an experience. We found
a sailor's haunt with gruff dark men and hard red-lipstick women.
At the bar a couple flirted, until she pulled his collar, slipped an arm
through his, and shimmied out; discretely followed by a silent hulk.
Ten minutes later she and Hulk return, arm in arm, laughing. The man…
We whispered worries of his fate until closing time came in sudden
darkness, before lights dimmed, shutters down and locked in drinking.
Panicking on how to leave, alive, intact, our virgin bodies shaking in
our ignored innocence. Relieved when we discovered the toilets were
also an exit to the dank dark docks.

Pacific Quay—Garden Festival 1988

We were the extras, backdrop for the TV,
so that Charles and Di moved through cheering crowds,
no empty spaces, animation between the flowers,
hours of standing to be a few seconds of moving screen.

The cavalcade reached the far side of the dock,
boat to the steps, and they were on our bank,
not talking, not smiling, moving at speed,
no doubt running late, so who cares
if the waiting throng, see or are seen.

The children, at the maypole, who danced
for us, for them, to keep out the cold,
must wonder why they spent half a day
twisting and turning, to be ignored;
not even visible on the broadcast,
hidden beneath the tower, lost in the rush.
I remember their enthusiasm dying,
ending a long day of nothing.

And there was the husband and wife
on their day of hope. She supported
at the dock railing, too weak to move,
recovering from cancer, stationery.
She waited in vain to see her Princess.

She is dead, Diana is dead,
the Festival site is gone,
that moment in time is over,
except in my head where it replays
with Charles and Di extras,
backdrop to things that did matter.

Gallowhill Road

In
the
fifties
We would stand on Gallow Hill
looking to the scaffold of cranes Goose neck
swan neck hammer head lining the river from Broomielaw
through Govan and down to John Brown's Dad pointing out Blythswood
where he worked proud of the berths and cranes he had planned

ship
mat-
ernity
Every summer Sunday
a walk to check on the funnels superstructures
rising on vessels progressing to the day they would launch
greeted by cacophonous horns bellowing triumph at another proudly Clyde-built
destroyer freighter ore-carrier tanker liner successful delivery of hull to river

in
the
sixties
a decade of closures
eleven shipyards gone to the breakers
Denny Harland and Woolf Stephens Simons
Lobnitz Scott and Sons and deepest felt by me Blythswood
the cranes skeletal fingers no longer clawing a blue sky

Diving Shipwrecks

You and Me Dad-we have done our time diving shipwrecks

George Wallace

What age was I, eight nine?
Does it matter? It was you, me and Allan, Robert,
going to see where you worked.
I never asked, but guess they had been before,
but not I, until that day, sixty years ago, or more.
Depends when this is read. Or should it be when I write it?
Does it matter? It is a memory every son wants
of his father, of the place where he earned the money,
that paid for ice creams, the big wooden yo-yo, for the bike
and the weekly comics, for the holidays on Arran.
I knew all this, for Mum told me, told me of the hours,
the study, told me of your right hand so much larger than your left
from hard labour from when you were fourteen.
Does it matter? That I remember the men boiler-suited grim
but laughing. The noise, so I could not hear the swearing,
though, in those distant days, I doubt they swore when I was there.
You didn't swear when women or children were in earshot.
Does it matter? That I remember the Board Room, all dark wood
walls, polished table and special chair with arms and higher back
for the owner, the man who owned your job, your time.
Does it matter, Dad? That I see you young, see me small
and know this never changed. No matter the shipyard went.
The job went. You went. Mum went. All slipped under the years,
the seas that drown us all. Does it matter? That I rarely swim down
into those reefs of childhood. You made a boat for me, handed me the oars,
said, the horizon is yours, and I rowed over the lip of the world
into…

21

The Ferryman at Blythswood

in my teenage years
the brass pocket watch
sat on its faux-velvet stand
on my bed-side table

Not really a stand
meant to be on a wall
with velvet to cushion
the motion of the river

this was the ferryman's
whose routine task was to ply
between North and South Yards
in the small open boat

on launch days he checked the time
chugged to the middle of the river
I was fascinated by the power
of a small open boat

the ferryman with his red flag
stopping river traffic
as if he held back the river itself
for the ship to be christened

Renfrew Ferry

there was a buzz of excitement
as I waited to cross or to meet dad
as he returned from work

pulled across on two heavy chains
which sank to the river bottom as the ferry
moved to leave clear passage for shipping

As it clanked its way you saw the power
of tidal surge and river flow as it curved
up or down stream struggling to hold its course

the chains were held in two channels on the ramps
set in the stones covered by metal plates
and with steel rods to stop them springing free

tension on the chains as the ferry approached
caused them to break to the surface dripping and angry
vibrating and fighting river or tide

Dad warned me to keep high on the ramp
of a chain which snapped at its weakest link
to whip from its tethers like a wild snake

it thrashed across the stones into the men
nearest the water amputating a man's leg
where crowds still pushed down to be first

A Renfrew Ferry Hogmanay

The crew thought as a ship Licensing Laws did not apply
so one Hogmanay they partied midstream and refused to budge
were boarded and arrested for being drunk in charge of a ferry

Tribute to The River Cart

'There is a cart which runs through Paisley without wheels.'
Dad's joke, repeated often when I was young,
did make me smile. This is the White Cart, on its long
meander down through Pollock and passed the Mills,
to meet, at Renfrew, it's Black Cart twin, Lochwinnoch born.
The river mouth gives the Clyde that necessary width,
crucial for those great Queens, Mary and Elizabeth,
HMS Vanguard, and all the rest from John Brown's.
Without The Cart would Clyde shipyards have attained
such fame? It is the Great Ships which made her name,
the glamour of the liners, the Pride of the Fleet,
until demand for ever larger vessels ordained
even Clyde and Cart together had not the scope, so came
decline and closures; the Yards no longer could compete.

Slack Water—Erskine Bridge 1969

Aftermath of the Barbecue, the river shining moon liquid, is at rest.
The concrete skeleton of the new bridge rises above us. Its unopened
roadway stretches the sky. Like ants we scurry to remove our presence,
douse the last flames, gather litter and beer cans, as if needed to feed
offspring waiting to be born, in future times and sullen towns.
All the casualties of exuberance and folk music, have been rescued
by sober drivers, are returning to Christian homes. not too much virtue
and innocence has fallen on grass and sand, along with bacon fat, alcohol,
those odd cigarettes. The Minister, our allotted chaperone of rectitude, who
does not believe in God, has slipped away. Pleading he needs time to write
his Sunday sermon, chose empty hymns.
We stare into the enamel bucket we used to heat soup. The inside is now shiny
steel to the level reached by Heinz cream of chicken. We pray the dissolved
lining does not kill anyone, thank God at least both were cream. We take a vow
of silence, promise never to speak of this.
An anguished cry spins us back to the river where the Police Superintendent's
daughter has been crushing cans. The Clyde sparkles with her thrown stars.
Tenant's, McEwans, Carlsberg, Skol, refusing to drown, now a constellation
lazily shimmering. After much swearing and laughter, we persuade her to stop
feeding more evidence of our debauchery to the slack water. We stuff the last
debris into our cars, drive back to Paisley, stopping at every empty litter-bin
filling with our empties.

Langbank

Like drowned fences they line the mud flats
appearing and disappearing with the tide
further out the channel buoys and lights
where the dredgers keep Glasgow accessible
to the merchant ships bringing wealth

these were the seasoning ponds
from a time before steel before steam
lying a forest of felled trees
timber soaked and dried by the ebb and flow
until seasoned wood for the shipyards
taken on the river to be crafted
into schooner and clippers, perhaps
the bones of Cutty Sark lay naked here
waiting for shipwrights' of Dumbarton adze
to craft her curves.

Bowling Harbour—1985

hard to think of this as once
an active place of business
barges coming and going

goods arriving from the river
to be transported to Glasgow
and onwards to the East Coast

now a gaggle of house-boats
bathe in the summer sun
some with peeling paint

others looking smart and bright
pride and joy of office workers
washing fluttering like flags

the impressive Custom House
dominates the harbour
I can see money was spent

this how importance declines
sinks into the mud and silt
the purpose becomes distant

but there is a glory here
beyond the harbour the river
water glistening blue

I am wrapped timeless floating
lured by the romance of vessels
at home in a safe harbour

The Lady Anne

at Rhu, Regatta of yachts built to the designs of Wm Fife III

She lies at rest, lovers gone
to recharge, while she awaits their return.
She sings quietly, occasionally sways
to show more of a white curve, glimpse
of her racy youth, a seductive exposure.

Smoothness draws the hand to touch
but she is another's, forbidden fruit,
this sailors' mistress, this dancer of the waves.

No God made this beauty, mans' work
before plastic. Crafted with passion
The Lady Anne.

Greenock Esplanade

heat radiates from the pavement
water kisses against the embankment
a perfect day to show off the Clyde
to our Canadian Visitors

We stop at the yellow pillar
explain it marks the deep water
at The Tail of the Bank
The Hole where the large ships
waited at anchor before going on
to the Glasgow docks

I point out the sweep
of distant mountains
how we can look back
up river towards Dumbarton
across to Helensburgh and Rhu

Sunken hull of the Captayanis
visible on this clear day
I tell how it sank when I worked
in the Building we can see ahead
the myth that locals spirited away
a massive propeller in open boats

I realise one of the boys
is not looking or listening
bent over close to the ground
clicks of multiple pictures
my Aunt asks him what
is so exciting

Ants he says
look at the ants
isn't this great
I can't wait
to show Dad

Bay Hotel Gourock

The Nineteen-sixties were heady days
American sailors over from the Holy Loch
Train loads of Glasgow girls
hunting down a good time

a flashy Yank far from home
spending the lonely dollars
homing in on a target
to hell with tomorrow

Who thinks Nuclear wipe-out
when skin full of Heavy beer
the Firth glistens silver
everyone becomes beautiful

James Dean's meeting Natalie Wood's
dreams of stars and the earth moving
lets jive and jitterbug till dawn
'another whisky sour, Mac'

of all the joints
in all the world
honey beehives
brylcreem quiff

USA and Scotland
another Special Relationship

Wemyss Bay Station and Pier

I had no time
for the glorious wooden curve
of building which linked
Station to pier

this was a racetrack
down hill from train
to catch the Clyde Steamer
Allan Robert and I sprinting

Allan would make the most
of our day with the Rover ticket
and there was never enough time
to fit our ambitions

Worse was carrying your case
going on holiday to Arran
the hordes in summer clothes
which meant men without ties
and women in cotton frocks
racing families to the pier

where we stood a sardine patience
with those nearest the edge praying
we did not all breathe in at the same
time or they would be swimming
to the island

and worse still the return
for that was uphill and the train
did not wait and your Mum your Dad
your brothers did not look back
confident if they made it in time so
would you

With My Brother at Largs

For Dr Allan P Walker

I go sudden into his enthusiasm
cynic voices drowned by his breaking smile
we'll see the yachts on the measured mile
and all the Clyde will glisten in the sun
he takes such pleasure reminding me of Fife
whose craft bring joy are treasured for their lines
today they'll sail where made in better times
he reels their names until they have a life
this is a day I'll not forget nor how
he buys me coffee and a bacon roll
says I'm glad you came aren't these the best
we munch salt and smoke and now
a warmth comes and lights my soul
with memories of how we laugh and jest

On the Next Tide – Largs Marina

A piper strides the wind to blow a Scottish air
as the yacht begins its journey to the Firth.
A squall threatens to collapse the umbrellas
of friends huddled in lea of beached boats.

Bunting in the rigging fights another gust,
a Pennant flutters bravely at the mizzen mast.
Teak, bulwarks, cockpit rail, round the transom,
conjure visions of Spanish Galleons, Drake and Hind,

a merchant adventurer, launched today in the Clyde
ready to ply every ocean, carry a captain's treasures,
the detailing on the hull reflects the glories aboard,
wood-lined caresses of cockpit and cabin,

the craft in fitting-out this Colvic hull, which sways
its passage between our cheers, as we fall in
to march behind, drookit, laughing, and alive.
Suddenly a shaft of sun and the gale subsides,

a swelling chorus of Hoorays, champagne christens
across her bow. Lowered, she settles, square and true,
in her home waters. The launch of one man's vision
to sail tomorrow and tomorrow and promises anew.

Arran Peaks

Built into the waves of life
How do those mountains become mine
I see them from the beach at Seamill
With memories of you on the sand
The dogs in the sea and sunset
Those ridges cut
Into the blue
Blaze in the dusk blood
Fade in the mists

Always the Arran peaks
Horizon of my being
Childhood on the Clyde steamers
Family summer holidays at Whiting Bay
Visits to my brother at High Corrie
Looking from Millport to Goat Fell
Recollections of a yacht in Lamlash Bay
A beach and sandcastles
The building of my hopes and dreams
How do I define a view
A foundation.

Seamill Shore

March 28th 2018 10.45am

dark red
blood red
lying on these rocks
nine dead roses
to be taken
on the next tide

blood red
dark red
heart broken
on these rocks
twelve dead years
waiting to be taken

blood red
dark red
coat on a stranger
approaching these rocks
coat on a ghost
today adrift

dark red
blood red
nine roses

For the Silent Curlew of My Beach

are you a harbinger of storm
grey feathered on this March morning
on the beach behind the Waterside Hotel
I am alone with you

ten pink roses which I think
match our wedding flowers
and who is to tell me otherwise
purple-red alstroemeria for contrast
peep from my bag-for-life

why do you not call as I approach
nor pick among the debris of winter tides
stand watchful   waiting
and I have hopes

which rise and fly with you
on reluctant wings
over receding waves
over the rock where I will scatter blooms
wonder why I talk to rock

and if you came

Hunterston A from Millport, Nineteen-fifties

blue-black night
oil polished sea
unearthly still broken
by a thunderous downpour

in the pillared bay window
on the upper floor of a Victorian villa
high above the town
eating cold mince sandwiches for supper

I love the rain-washed glass
clear crisp broken lightning
slicing the horizon to light up
the half-built power station

each flash pulls me to the dark
staring through storm plunged glass
which does not silence a howling wind
the room behind bright with electricity

I want to stand in the cleansing
deluge and laugh at other's fear
the white shape of Hunterston A
flickers like a B-movie monster

Millport—Wish you were here

a black and white picture of the old town
three children with ice cream
thirties snapshot of seaside frolics
tickles nostalgia

tonight you ignore the peeling paint
gull splattered pavement
detritus of day-trippers
the promenade grey concrete desolate
evening drizzle mingles with salt spray

The faded pub sign creaks
a shaft of light cuts the pavement
as a karaoke 'How many roads' shuffles out
in the bus shelter you scribble postcards

wishing distant relatives
long parted friends
were here
a tick off the list
proving you belong somewhere

Out-going Tide—Rothesay

I linger at the rock pool,
step back into childhood.
The day changes overhead
warm then cold on my bent back.

The view alters with the sky;
reflections shut me out,
until shadows skid across
reopening the scenes below.

Bright red anemones at the waterline,
a crab, size of a finger-nail, scuttles,
pincers pull at shreds of sea-weed
as water-boatmen skim above.

A sea-breeze creases between the rocks,
whispering old names, talking of Arran,
Bute, Cumbrae, Ailsa Craig
summers on the Clyde.

The thrum of a diesel engine,
the sharp cry of gulls trailing astern,
pulls me from the enclosed space,
eyes lifting to the beach,

draped with a necklace of seaweed,
bejewelled with shiny cans,
trimmed with plastic.

Kilchattan—Isle of Bute

The sun must still shine on Kilchattan, but
I have never returned to the bay
where the sand was warm, the breeze was gentle.
The water pale blue to the shelf, dark blue

thereafter, as warning of drowning, of
body trapped to reappear long after tears
had dried.   The safety warning for the run
through singing wavelets of our Bute holiday

before chilly float in the Firth
the rush up the beach to be rough towelled
before settling with sun and book
to dreams of exotic mysteries

Sheltered nook among the spiky grass,
dunes embraced, while on the strand a family
played.   Two downs-syndrome children laughed,
smiled. Their Mum and Dad organized the cricket.

Initiation to a world of difference,
of another sun.   A changed perception.

Jupiter

Paddle-steamer Jupiter in pursuit of The Royal Yacht Britannia down The Firth from Kilchattan Bay Bute

I feel the shock, wood on water,
air vibrating,
rolling through the bracken.
Thud thud thud
of surface tension broken.
My heart races in time,
Beat beat beat
an inner smile breaking.
Then she is seen, paddles flailing, white wave
spreading from her bow.   Water surging from paddle boxes.
All rawness

Further out The Royal Yacht slips on.
The reason for the Old Lady lifting her skirts
to schottische out from Kilchattan Bay.
She cannot catch, too old and slow,
not the breeding.
Yet the kicking heels, rasped breath,
a fading beauty in full flight,
is the victor.

Holidays at Whiting Bay—Arran

We would come down from the guest-house,   walk along the front
towards the beach. There was a little row of shops: ice-cream shop,
gift shop, bric-a-brac, a desire to buy something, to get the lemon
cubes, the little knife; which I took up into the square   nearly cut
the end off my finger, although Dad had said   be careful with that
and I was   but I wasn't   the blood   and fear   Dad holding it
wrapping a hankie round it   assuring me that it would be OK

We made the journey on past   hotels   grass   the cricket match
wandering down bye-ways   through the dunes out onto the beach
Finding the secluded cove after walking for what seemed like miles
but wasn't   Laid out the travel rug   built sand-castles dug tunnels

This was our holiday   this was what I wanted   for every year
to come here   and having frozen   the wind blowing through me
when I came out of the sea towel roughly rubbed over me I would
read a book   watch the clouds drift by   making patterns   Patterns
in which I could see other worlds

At Lochranza Distillery

In the shadow of The Sleeping Warrior
I indulge my dreams.
Arran rolls on the tongue,
breathe in the aroma of malt, land, sea
matured in the ages of Scotland.

It is said the island is Scotland in miniature,
from the Highlands of Goatfell,
a central belt of the String Road,
to the lowlands of Kildonan and Lagg,
a place of myth and of spirits.

On Machrie Moor stone circles, burial cairns,
a link to our past, time had no meaning
as I surveyed those ancient stones,
wondered if Bruce also found inspiration here
before seeking safety in the King's Cave.

At Lochranza, necromancy conjures water and barley
memories of ancestors and hopes for tomorrow,
holidays and sunshine distilled into liquid.
I raise a glass, amber pure
taste past, present,

the ferry dances sunlit waves
as it crosses the Kilbrannan Sound
river merging with the Atlantic
cradled in my hand
the water of life.

Sunset: Arran

the sun plunges
sprays a fire-gold halo
Arran turns charcoal black

Goat Fell
shadow mountain mystery
against the burning sky

this eruption of light
splendour beyond
dream

the Firth glows
clouds bleed
with delight

on the beach
I wait for dark
to deep-blue the heavens

I gaze to stars
waters swish moon silver
beautiful

sing love songs
to the night

Ailsa Craig

    – volcanic plug – curlers granite – gannet's haven
    – fairy rock – emigrants' farewell to the Clyde
    – an Irish Giant's parting shot at his Scottish rival
    – Paddy's Milestone – the furthest Clyde steamers
       took day trippers – end of my journey